Stories for Christmas

I Talk You Talk Press

CONTENTS

INTRODUCTION

There are five short Christmas stories for learners of English in this book.

1. A CHRISTMAS PRESENT FOR CARA

"Another drink, Rick?" asked Justin.

Rick looked at his watch. "I don't know…I have to buy my wife's Christmas present. It's Christmas Eve, and I still haven't bought her anything."

"Oh go on. Just one more drink," said Justin. "I'm buying."

Rick looked at Justin and smiled. "Oh, OK. Just one."

It was 4:00pm on Christmas Eve in Dublin. Rick and Justin had been in the pub all day.

I wonder what time the shops close today, thought Rick. *I'm sure they are open late for Christmas shopping.*

He looked through the window at the shops outside. The lights were still on.

Justin came back to the table with two pints of beer.

"It looks cold out there," said Justin. "It's much better in here, with a nice warm fire, Christmas music and beer."

"I agree," said Rick. He picked up his beer and drank some. "Ooh, that's nice."

"So, what are you going to buy Cara for Christmas?" asked Justin.

"I'm going to buy her a necklace. I looked in the jewellery shop window yesterday. They had some nice necklaces," said Rick. "And she said she wanted jewellery."

Ted, Rick's friend, came into the pub. He sat with Rick and Justin and they talked for a long time. Ted bought some more beer for everyone. Rick was feeling drunk, but very happy. It was Christmas Eve and he was drinking in a warm pub with his friends.

Then, he remembered. "What time is it?"

Justin looked at his watch. "It's seven thirty," he said.

Rick looked out of the window. "The shops are closed!" he shouted. He put his coat and his hat on quickly. "I have to buy a present for Cara!"

Justin stood up. "I'll come with you," he said. "I promised my wife I would be home early today."

Rick and Justin said goodbye to Ted and walked out of the pub into the cold snowy night.

Rick looked around. "Oh no! The jewellery shop is closed! Everywhere is closed! What am I going to do?"

Justin walked around the corner. "There's a light on over there. I think that's a hardware shop. It might still be open."

"Hardware shop? What can I buy for my wife in a hardware shop?!" asked Rick. "She likes jewellery, not tools!"

"You might find something nice," said Justin. "They sell many things."

Rick and Justin hurried to the hardware shop.

"It's open!" said Rick. "I hope I can get something nice."

They walked into the shop and looked around. There were tools, paints and gardening equipment.

"How about a hammer?" asked Justin. He picked it up and looked at it carefully.

"I don't think she wants a hammer," said Rick.

"She could use it to hit you," said Justin.

"Justin, shut up! You're drunk!" shouted Rick.

"You're drunk, too," said Justin.

"I know," said Rick. "And my head hurts. But if I don't buy Cara a Christmas present, her mother will be very angry, and then my head will really hurt!"

Justin and Rick walked into the gardening area.

"How about some gardening boots?" asked Justin.

"We don't have a garden," said Rick.

They walked to the other corner of the shop.

"This is perfect!" said Justin. "A camping stove!"

He picked the camping stove up and gave it to Rick.

"Really? Do you think so?" asked Rick. "Cara doesn't go camping."

"No, but she likes cooking! It's a great present!" said Justin.

Rick was feeling very drunk. He couldn't think clearly.

"Yeah, you're right! Cara loves cooking!" he said.

He paid for the stove and they walked out of the shop.

Rick walked home in a very happy mood. He had enjoyed a nice evening with his friends, and he had bought his wife a present.

It was Christmas morning. Rick woke up early. He had a headache.

It's Christmas morning! he thought. He looked at Cara. She was still sleeping.

I hope she likes her necklace, he thought. Then, he remembered.

Oh no! I didn't buy her a necklace! I bought her a camping stove! I still have to wrap it up.

He got out of bed and went downstairs. He took the camping stove into the living room and wrapped it up in red and green wrapping paper. He put it under the tree.

She will be so angry, he thought. *She wanted a necklace. I hope she opens the present before her parents come for dinner.*

Cara got up. "Merry Christmas Rick!" she said. "Did you have a nice time with Justin last night?"

"Oh yes," said Rick. "Cara, do you want to open your present?"

"Now? I've just got up. It's too early. Let's wait. My parents are coming for dinner. We can open our presents then," said Cara. She looked under the tree. "Oh, that's a big box. I wonder what it is?"

Oh no! thought Rick. *She will open the present in front of her mother and father! She will be so disappointed!*

Cara was busy all morning. She was making Christmas dinner. Then, at 1:00pm, there was a knock at the door.

Rick went to open the door.

"Merry Christmas, Rick!" said Cara's mother and father. Cara's mother hugged him and her father shook his hand.

They had lots of presents. They went into the living room and sat down. Just then, Cara shouted, "No! I don't believe it!"

Rick ran into the kitchen. "What is it?" he said. "What's wrong?"

Cara was standing at the gas stove. She was switching it on and off.

"There's no gas! I can't use the stove! I can't boil the vegetables!"

Rick looked at the gas stove. He tried switching it on and off, but it was broken.

"What about the turkey?" he asked.

"The turkey is done," said Cara. "But what am I going to do? We can't just eat turkey. It's Christmas! What about the vegetables?"

"Is everything OK?" asked Cara's mother. She walked into the kitchen and hugged Cara.

"The stove is broken," said Cara. "What are we going to do?"

"Well, let's go into the living room and open our presents first. We can think about the stove later," said Cara's mother.

They all walked into the living room and sat down.

Cara looked at Rick.

"Rick, why are you smiling? You look very happy."

Rick walked over to the Christmas tree and picked up the box.

"This is for you Cara. It's the perfect present for you today."

Cara took the present. "It's very heavy," she said. She opened it and took it out of the box.

"Oh Rick! It's a camping stove! I don't believe it! This really is perfect! Now I can boil the vegetables and we can have a real Christmas dinner!" she said. She kissed Rick on the cheek.

Cara's mother and father smiled.

"But, I don't understand. How did you know that I would need a stove today?" asked Cara.

"Oh, well, you know," said Rick. "I just had a feeling."

"It's a sign," said Cara's mother. "A sign that he loves you very much Cara."

"Oh Rick, you really are the perfect husband!" said Cara. "This is so much better than jewellery!"

Rick smiled. He stood up and walked towards the kitchen. "Champagne, anyone?" he said.

2. ALZBETA'S TABLE

Alzbeta is polishing the wooden table in her living room. It's a large table. It's big enough for six people, but two extra pieces are hidden under the table. If you pull them out, the table is big enough for twelve people. Alzbeta's husband, Stan, was a clever woodworker. He built the table after they arrived in America from Poland. They had a very small house then, but Stan said, "We are a family. The family will grow. I will work hard, and we will have a bigger house."

Of course, Stan was right. They had four children. The table is 60 years old now.

"This is your sixty-first Christmas," Alzbeta tells the table. She laughs at herself. *You crazy old lady! Talking to a table!*

She has just moved into a large home unit in a retirement village. The village is very good. Alzbeta can cook for herself, or eat in the central dining room. Every day there are events like bingo, or singing, or exercise classes. She can join the chorus, the lawn bowls club, the card group, or the quilting circle. She only moved to the village two weeks ago, so she hasn't joined anything yet.

The table is really too big and heavy for Alzbeta's new house, but she wanted to bring it with her. She thinks that all the relatives, children and friends who sat down to eat at her table have left something of themselves behind. The old polished wood holds so many memories. Some are very happy, and others are sad, but they are all her memories.

All the meals I cooked, she thinks. *And all the people who ate them. Well, this year will be different. I have no one to cook for.*

The family had gathered at the end of November. They travelled from all over America and overseas to celebrate a last Thanksgiving in the family home. They packed up the house, and helped Alzbeta get ready to move to the retirement village. She didn't want to sell the big old house, but it was too difficult for her to look after it alone.

Everyone asked Alzbeta to spend Christmas with them.

"No," she said. "I want to stay in my new house. I want to meet my new neighbours. I don't want to travel."

So tomorrow she will eat Christmas dinner in the central dining room in the village. She will meet some of her new neighbours. All the residents who will be alone at Christmas will be there.

But today, she feels restless and lonely.

It's Christmas Eve, and I'm not cooking. That's why I feel strange. Usually I was so busy, thought Alzbeta.

Alzbeta and Stan kept their Polish family traditions alive in America. Every Christmas Eve Alzbeta served twelve different dishes. The children watched the sky. When the first star appeared, everyone sat at the table and shared the thin white Christmas bread. Then they ate a feast of fish and vegetables.

Alzbeta decides she will cook something special. She will make one of the recipes she always cooked for Christmas Eve.

Mushroom soup, she thinks. *I will make mushroom soup. I will sit at the table tonight, and eat my soup and remember.*

She feels much better. An hour later the kitchen smells wonderful. Alzbeta has used a mixture of both fresh and dried mushrooms. Later she will add sour cream and noodles.

The doorbell rings. Alzbeta goes to answer it. A thin man in a heavy jacket is standing outside the door.

"Hello, Alzbeta. I'd like to introduce myself. I'm called Matt. I'm a member of the village welcome committee. I'm sorry that I have not been able to come to see you before. Is everything OK? Can I help you with anything?"

"Everything is fine, thank you."

"Will you join us for Christmas dinner tomorrow?" asks Matt.

"Yes, I will. My family all live far away. So yes, I will come. See you tomorrow," she says.

"Great," says Matt. But he doesn't go away. He is sniffing.

"Is there something wrong?" asks Alzbeta.

"I'm sorry. I can smell something delicious. Are you making

mushroom soup?"

"Yes. I always make it on Christmas Eve."

"It smells like the soup my wife used to make. I miss it. I miss her."

"It's not ready yet. But would you like to come back later? I will give you some."

Matt looks delighted. "Yes please!" Then he looks a little sad. "But would it be OK if I came to have the soup with you? I will feel very lonely if I eat it on my own."

Alzbeta is not sure. "Uh, I don't know."

"I know a very good Polish bakery. I will bring some fine bread. Please say yes."

This is a little crazy, but why not? The table and I will have company after all, she thinks.

Alzbeta laughs. "OK. You can come," she says. "Just before the stars come out. Come then."

"Yes, I know. We will eat after the first star appears." Matt stands up very straight. He bows in an old-fashioned European way. "Mateusz Adamski at your service." He goes away.

Alzbeta closes the door, and goes back to the kitchen. Her husband, Stan was a very big man, but this small thin man still reminds her of him, somehow. She will enjoy having a little company tonight.

It's lunchtime, so she makes herself a sandwich and sits down to watch television. The house is very clean, but during the afternoon she cleans it again. She checks her computer. The sun will set at 5:00pm. The first stars will appear after that. She makes some old-fashioned square noodles. Then she finds a beautiful white tablecloth, and lays the table. She heats the soup and throws the noodles into the pot.

It is 4:45pm when her doorbell rings.

He's early, she thinks.

She opens the door. Mateusz is there. He is carrying a basket of bread. He looks embarrassed. "I'm early because we must be ready when the first star appears. And you see, I thought … Well, I told a few people that you were making mushroom soup, and they all wanted to come."

A group of people were standing behind Mateusz.

"Come in," says Alzbeta. She is panicking. She has made a big pot of soup, but there are a lot of people.

Mateusz stands by the door, and introduces everyone as they walk in.

"Dagmara, Marika, Albert, Bernard, Felix, Julia, Karol, Konrad, Stefania and Ada."

Suddenly, the room is full of people. Everyone is smiling. Alzbeta sees that everyone is carrying food.

"Matt told us that you were making mushroom soup," says one of the women. Alzbeta thinks her name is Dagmara. "We all thought about our families, and felt a little sad. Then I thought, if she can do it, we can too. It was a rush to buy ingredients and cook, but we managed it. All together we are twelve people, so we have twelve dishes."

"Hurry!" says one of the men. "We don't have much time. Everything must be ready before the first star. Where can we put the food? Do you have enough room?"

Alzbeta proudly shows them her table. Everyone helps. The table is pulled out to its full size. Now twelve people can sit around it. Someone runs to their house and brings more chairs.

They all sit. Karol, a very tall man with a big moustache, proudly puts Christmas wafers on the table. "My sister in Warsaw sends them to me." Everyone breaks off pieces of the thin bread, and shares them with other people at the table. They exchange good wishes and greetings. Then it's time to eat.

It is a wonderful party. Tomorrow they will eat traditional American food – turkey, sweet potatoes and cranberry sauce. But tonight, they eat trout, herring, salmon, sauerkraut, potato croquettes, dumplings, poppy seed bread, rye bread, little cheese pies, beets, and dried fruit. They speak in a mixture of English and Polish. They tell jokes, and share memories and stories.

After the party, everyone helps to clean up.

Then they are leaving.

"See you tomorrow!"

"We must do this again."

"You must give me your recipe for the potato croquettes."

Mateusz is the last person to leave. "Welcome to our village. I am very pleased you came to live here."

He bows, and disappears into the cold dark night.

Alone in her house, Alzbeta pats the table.

"I still need you," she says. "I hope there is still enough room in that old wood for some more memories."

3. THE CHRISTMAS TREE

It was three days before Christmas. Sam and Jessica were driving to the garden centre. It was a cold evening. The fields and forest around the road were white with snow and frost.

"I hope there are some nice Christmas trees left at the garden centre," said Jessica.

"Yes," said Sam. "It is very late. But we have both been very busy at work. We couldn't buy one earlier. But don't worry. I'm sure there will be some left."

"A big Christmas tree will look wonderful in our living room," said Jessica. "We need some lights too. Let's get some lights at the general store before we go to the garden centre."

Sam and Jessica stopped at the general store and chose some big, colourful Christmas tree lights. Then they drove to the garden centre and parked the car near the entrance.

They walked into the garden centre and looked around.

"Sam, where are the Christmas trees?" asked Jessica.

Sam looked around. "I don't know," he said. "I'll ask that salesman over there."

They walked over to the salesman standing near the cash register.

"Excuse me," said Sam. "Where are the Christmas trees?"

"I'm sorry," said the man. "You are too late. We are sold out."

"Sold out?!" said Jessica. "But, we need a Christmas tree!"

"I'm sorry," said the salesman. "It's very late."

"Are you going to get any more trees in before Christmas?" asked Jessica.

"No, I'm sorry," said the salesman. "We had many trees but we sold them already. We are not going to get any more. It's Christmas Eve tomorrow. We are closed from tomorrow to December twenty-seventh."

Another man walked over to the salesman.

"Excuse me," he said. "Where are the Christmas trees?"

"I'm sorry," said the salesman. "We are sold out."

"Oh no!" said the man. He put his head in his hands. "The children in the hospital will be so sad! They have no Christmas tree yet. I came here from the next town. The garden centre in the next town has also sold out. We've been so busy this year. We had no time to get a tree. We usually get one in early December, but some of our staff were ill and…Oh no!"

"I'm sorry," said the salesman.

Sam and Jessica walked out of the shop and got back in their car.

"So we have no Christmas tree this year," said Jessica sadly.

"No Christmas tree," said Sam, shaking his head. "And the children at the hospital don't have a Christmas tree either."

"That's sad," said Jessica.

"Yes, it is. Oh well, let's go home," said Sam. He started the engine and they drove out of the car park.

They drove along the dark country road. There were no other cars on the road. Jessica looked out of the window into the darkness. Then, she had an idea.

"Sam, there is a forest over there," she said.

"And?"

"Well, there are trees in the forest," said Jessica.

Sam and Jessica looked at each other.

"And there are no other cars on the road," said Sam.

"So no one will see us," said Jessica. "Where's the chainsaw?"

"It's in the garage," said Sam. "Let's go home and pick it up."

Sam and Jessica drove home. Jessica waited in the car while Sam went into the garage to get the chainsaw and a torch. He put everything in the boot of the car.

"Let's go," said Sam.

They drove back along the dark, empty road. They stopped at the side of the road near the forest.

"Come on, let's be quick," said Sam.

They got out of the car and walked through the snowy field. They soon came to the edge of the forest.

"Who owns this forest Sam?" asked Jessica.

"I don't know," said Sam. "The government, maybe? But it's OK. There are so many trees. The forest owner won't notice if one tree is missing."

Sam shone the torch light onto the trees.

"Which one?" he asked.

"They all look the same," said Jessica. "But how about this one? It's not too big, so we can carry it easily."

"OK," said Sam. "Let's be quick."

Jessica held the torch and Sam chopped the tree down with the chainsaw. It didn't take long. It fell heavily onto the ground.

"Let's go," said Sam.

Jessica held the top of the tree, and Sam held the bottom of the tree. They picked it up and started walking.

"It's heavy," said Jessica.

"I know, but the car isn't so far away. Quick, let's hurry," said Sam.

They walked slowly through the snowy field carrying the tree.

"Look! There's a car!" said Jessica.

Sam looked over at the road.

"And there's another one!" said Sam. "Why are there so many cars on the road at this time?"

"I hope they don't see us stealing this tree," said Jessica.

They walked towards the car. Then, a small truck on the road slowed down.

"Oh no, there's a man. He's looking at us," said Jessica.

The truck stopped next to their car.

"Oh no! He's stopping! What should we say?" said Jessica.

"I don't know," said Sam.

"He might be the forest owner!" said Jessica. "He might call the police!"

The truck driver got out of his truck. He was a tall man and he was wearing work clothes. He looked like a farm worker.

"Do you need some help?" he said.

"Oh, er, no. It's OK. We are nearly at the car," said Sam.

"Have you had a busy Christmas season? I think Christmas tree farmers have been very busy this year."

"Christmas tree farmers?" said Jessica.

"Oh yes," said Sam quickly. "We have been very busy."

"That's good for business!" said the man. He looked at Sam and Jessica's car. "Don't you have a truck?"

"Er, yes, but er…the truck broke down last night. It needs some repairs," said Sam.

"Bad timing! So where are you taking this tree?" asked the truck driver. "Who has ordered this tree so late?"

"Oh, er…the hospital. The children's hospital in the next town," said Sam.

"Really? That's lucky. I'm going to the next town. I live there. I can take it for you," said the man.

"No, no. It's OK. We can take it ourselves," said Sam.

"No. Your car is too small. Put the tree in my truck. I can take it to the hospital," said the truck driver.

He was a strong man. He took the end of the tree from Jessica and lifted it into his truck.

"I'll follow you," he said to Sam and Jessica.

Sam and Jessica got back into their car.

"Jessica, do you know where the children's hospital is?" asked Sam.

"No. Do you?" asked Jessica.

"No," said Sam. "Check the map on your mobile phone."

"My phone battery is dead," said Jessica. "Maybe there are road signs?"

They drove through the snow to the next town. It took 30 minutes. There were no signs to the hospital.

"Which way?" asked Sam.

"I don't know," said Jessica. "Left?"

They drove down the main street and turned left.

The truck driver sounded his horn. Sam stopped the car and looked out of the window.

"You're going the wrong way!" shouted the truck driver. "It's that way!" He pointed to a road on the right.

"Oh, right, yes. Sorry," said Sam.

At last, they arrived at the hospital.

"It's really small," said Jessica. "That's why there were no signs."

They parked in front of the main entrance and got out of the car.

A nurse saw them and came out of the hospital.

"Special delivery for you!" said the truck driver. He opened the truck doors. The nurse saw the tree.

"Oh thank you! Thank you! The children will be very happy!" she said. "This is the best Christmas present for the children! Thank you!"

The nurse looked at the truck driver, Sam and Jessica.

"Who are you? Do you work at the garden centre?"

"Christmas tree farmers!" said Sam, quickly. "Merry Christmas!" He got back in the car. Jessica followed him.

"Merry Christmas!" said Jessica. She looked at the truck driver. "And thank you for your help!"

They drove out of the car park. Behind them, the truck driver and the nurse watched them drive away.

"That wasn't part of our plan," said Sam.

"No, it wasn't," said Jessica.

"Let's go home. We have the Christmas tree lights. We can put them around the window," said Sam.

"That's a good idea," said Jessica. "We have the lights, and the children in the hospital have a Christmas tree. I think that's the best ending."

4. THE BRASS BAND GIRLS

Every Saturday afternoon in December, Lucy, Caroline, Julie and Alison played music in the centre of town. Lucy and Caroline played the trumpet, Julie played the horn, and Alison played the trombone. They stood in the main shopping street and played Christmas carols.

Everyone in the town loved their music. People stopped to listen to them and often said that their music gave the town a nice Christmas feel.

The girls were music students at the local university. They didn't have much money. When they played in the town centre, they put a trumpet case in front of them. Many people in the town threw money into the trumpet case. Most people gave them coins, but some people really loved their music and gave them banknotes. The people in town were happy because they could enjoy Christmas music while they were shopping. The girls were happy because they could get money, and it was fun to play music and make people happy.

One cold Saturday afternoon at around 4:00pm, the girls were standing outside a large supermarket. It was snowing and they were very cold.

"It's getting dark," said Lucy. "And it's very cold. Shall we finish?"

"We have been here since 10:00am. We have a lot of money. I think it's time to go," said Alison.

"Wait," said Caroline. "Look at that old woman over there."

The girls looked at the old woman. She was standing across the road and she was looking at them.

"She's waiting for us to start playing again," said Caroline.

"OK, let's play one more carol for her," said Lucy.

The girls started to play the carol, 'Silent Night'.

The old woman smiled. She crossed over the road and walked towards the girls. She stopped in front of the girls and the open trumpet case, and opened her handbag. She was looking for her purse. She wanted to give the girls some money.

Just then, a man ran across the road towards the old woman. He took her purse out of her bag and ran down the road into the crowds of shoppers.

The girls stopped playing. They shouted "Stop! Stop that man!" But the man was too fast. He ran away with the old woman's purse.

The old woman was very shocked. Alison put her arms around her. Lucy ran into the supermarket. She told the manager about the old woman. The manager called the police. Very soon the police came. They asked the girls and the old woman questions about the man. Then they took the old woman home.

"Will they catch the man?" Lucy asked the supermarket manager.

"I don't think so," she answered. "I'm afraid that old woman will not get her purse back."

The girls were very sad. It was a terrible end to a happy day.

"A man took her purse when she was giving us some money. It's terrible! The old woman was so kind to us, but this bad thing happened," said Lucy. "I feel so bad."

"What can we do?" asked Julie. "I want to help the old woman."

The girls put their musical instruments in their cases. Then, they put the money in a bag.

"What's that?" asked Alison.

There was an envelope on the ground. She picked it up.

"Maybe it fell out of the old woman's bag," said Caroline.

They opened it. It was a Christmas card. Alison read it.

---*To Eileen, Merry Christmas and a Happy New Year. From Frank.*---

"The old woman is called Eileen. So this is her address on the envelope," said Alison. "She doesn't live so far away. We can return it to her."

The girls went into a café in the shopping centre and ordered cups of cocoa. It was nice and warm in the café.

"OK, time to count the money," said Lucy. She took all the money out of the bag and spread it on the table.

The girls counted the money quietly. Other people sitting in the café watched them, smiling.

"This has been our best day," said Lucy. "We have two hundred pounds!"

The girls were very happy to get so much money, but they were also very sad. They couldn't stop thinking about the old woman.

"I have an idea," said Lucy. "Let's give some of the money to the old woman."

"That's a good idea," said Alison. "How much?"

The girls thought about it for a few seconds.

"How about half?" asked Julie.

"Yes! Let's give her half!" said Caroline. "Let's give her a hundred pounds. I think she will be very happy."

The next morning, Eileen Marsh was sitting in her living room eating beans on toast and drinking tea.

She heard something outside. She put her tea down on the table.

What's that? she thought. *It's Silent Night.*

She stood up and looked out of the window. There were four girls in her garden. Two were playing the trumpet, one was playing the horn and another was playing the trombone.

It's the girls from yesterday! she thought. *What are they doing here?*

She opened the front door. Other people in the street opened their doors and stood in their gardens, watching the girls playing. When they finished, everyone clapped.

Lucy walked towards the woman. She was carrying a Christmas present.

"This is for you, Eileen. Merry Christmas," she said.

"But, how did you find me?" asked Eileen.

Lucy gave her the card. "When that man took your purse, this card fell out of your bag," she said.

"Oh, thank you," said Eileen. "What's in the box?"

"It's a present for you," said Julie. "Open it."

"I can't open it here. It's too cold. Come inside," said Eileen.

The girls walked into Eileen's living room.

"Sit down," said Eileen. The girls sat down together on the sofa with their musical instruments on their knees.

Eileen sat down and opened the box carefully. Inside, there was an envelope.

"What's this?" she said.

"Open it," said Lucy.

Eileen opened it.

"Oh!" she said. She looked at the money. Then she looked at the girls.

"But, I can't take this money!" said Eileen. "Here, take it back."

Eileen stood up to give the money back, but the girls were too fast.

They stood up and ran out of the house, through the garden and down the road. When they reached the corner of the road, they turned around.

"Merry Christmas, Eileen!" they shouted.

Eileen smiled at them. "Merry Christmas! And thank you!"

Then, she went back inside and ate the rest of her beans on toast.

I'll be able to buy Christmas presents for my grandchildren after all, she thought.

5. THE BOY ON THE BEACH

Saturday

Kath loves the drive to the beach house. From the time the car turns off the main road, she feels that the holiday has begun. She leans forward looking out the front window of the car. There are tall pine trees on either side of the road, so she can't see the sea, but then the narrow road turns a corner, and there's the sea!

Ted parks the car next to a small four-roomed house, at the very end of the narrow road. Next to the house is an old caravan, and beyond the house and the caravan are the beach and the sea.

Kath and Ted Williams are the first to arrive this year. It's 23rd December. Christmas Day is on Monday this year, so everyone stopped work on Friday. They got up early, and packed their big, old car with food and clothes, and of course the Christmas presents. It takes about two and a half hours to drive from their home. Their daughter Marie, her husband Doug, and their three children will arrive sometime in the afternoon. Peter, Joanne, the twins and Stephanie, their eldest child, will come later. It takes them more than eight hours to drive up from Wellington. Peter will be tired from driving all day, but he won't mind. He has been coming to the beach house for Christmas every year since he was a very small boy. He can't imagine going anywhere else.

Ted and Kath open up the house and the caravan. No one has been here since Easter. There is sand everywhere. Ted sweeps it up, and opens all the windows. Kath turns on the refrigerators, and takes the plastic covers off the beds. They work hard. By the time Doug drives the station wagon through the gateway, Kath and Ted are sitting outside, drinking cups of tea.

The station wagon stops, and the children jump out.

"Gran! Granddad!" they shout. They run to their grandparents. Everyone hugs.

Marie and Doug follow them. They are smiling.

Marie leans down and kisses her mother. "Hi Mum." She looks at the old garden furniture arranged on the grass in front of the house. "You've been busy."

Doug and Ted shake hands.

"How was the drive?" Ted asks.

"Not too bad. Of course there was a lot of traffic, but no big problems," answers Doug. "We stopped at a McDonalds for lunch."

The children are throwing bags out of the station wagon and searching in them.

"What are you doing?" calls Kath.

"Swim suits, towels! We want to go for a swim!"

Marie laughs. "Wait a minute."

She goes over to help them find the swimsuits and towels. The children run into the house to change, and then they run down to the beach, shouting and laughing. Ted goes with them.

Kath makes another pot of tea. Doug and Marie sit down, and they watch the children running in and out of the water.

"It's good to be here," says Doug. "I need a holiday."

"Where are we all sleeping?" asks Marie.

"Well, the three girls can sleep in the caravan this year. They're older now, and I'm sure they will be OK out there. Peter is bringing a big tent. The boys can camp out too."

"Great. Tim will love it!" Marie thinks her mother's plan is very good.

Doug thinks so too. "So, only adults in the house! Heaven!"

"You can relax, Doug." Marie stands up. "I'm going to unpack the food from the car, and talk to Mum about menus."

The house has two big old refrigerators and a freezer. It is far from any supermarket, so Kath, Joanne and Marie bring most of the food they will eat with them.

When Peter and Joanne, Stephanie and the twins, Wills and Jamie arrive, the BBQ is lit, and there are piles of sausages waiting to be cooked. Bread, coleslaw and fruit are waiting on the table.

Ted grills sausages for the children, while Peter and Doug put up the tent. Amy, Beth and Tim have just come up from the beach. They are still wearing swimsuits. As it gets cooler, they put sweaters on.

"Where's the tomato sauce?" Wills cannot imagine eating sausages without tomato sauce.

"Tomato sauce! Oh, no! We forgot! We didn't bring any." Ted loves teasing his grandchildren.

Wills looks like he might cry. "Granddad!"

"The tomato sauce is coming!" calls his grandmother. "Don't tease the children, Ted!"

She comes out of the house with the tomato sauce. The children eat piles of food.

It is only 9:00pm, and it is not quite dark yet, but all the children are yawning.

"Bed," says Joanne.

"Yes, time for bed," says Marie.

"Oh, Mum!" say all the children.

"No arguing," says Marie. "You all look tired. You have been on the beach for hours, and Stephanie, Wills and Jamie have been travelling all day."

The children complain, but they are very sleepy. So Amy, Beth and Tim go to have showers to wash the sand and salt off. The beach house is very simple, but it has three showers. There are two in an outside bathroom, and another one inside the house. The girls climb into the caravan, and the boys get into the tent. The girls have bunk beds with mattresses, but the boys have rubber mats and sleeping bags.

The adults sit outside at the table as night falls. There is giggling and talking from the tent and the caravan. The cousins like each other very much. They are excited to be together. They are excited to be at the beach. And of course, tomorrow is Christmas Eve.

"Quiet!" shouts Doug. "Go to sleep!"

There is more giggling and laughing and then, finally, there is silence.

Kath starts to grill more sausages for the adults. Ted goes inside and brings out beer.

Peter pours himself a glass. He lies back in his chair and stretches his arms. "Heaven," he says.

Doug agrees, "This is the life. I'm never going back to the city."
Everyone laughs.

Sunday

"Dad, Dad!" Wills and Jamie are in the house. They are shaking their father to wake him up. "Can we go for a swim?"

Peter wakes up. "What time is it?" He looks at his watch. He groans. "Six o'clock! Go back to bed."

"Oh, Dad. We've been awake for hours! You wouldn't let us swim yesterday. You said it was too late."

"No way! You can't go anywhere near the water unless an adult is watching you. And I am not getting out of bed. Go and have some breakfast. I'll get up soon."

When Kath gets up at 7:30am, all the children are in the living room. Stephanie is making toast. The dining table is covered with cereal packets and crumbs. Wills' face is covered with tomato sauce.

"That's disgusting Wills," says Kath. "Why are you eating toast with tomato sauce on it?"

Stephanie sighs. "I know Gran. I told him not to. But he wouldn't have jam or honey."

"It tastes great, Gran," says Wills. "You should try it!"

"No thank you. Now who is going to help me clear up this mess?"

When everything is clean and tidy, Kath sends the children to shower, clean their teeth and dress.

Slowly, the other adults appear. Peter makes coffee. They eat toast.

Ted looks at the tide tables. He printed them from the Internet, and he has hung them on the wall. "If you want shellfish, you'll have to go soon," he says. "Low tide is at 9:00am."

Doug and Peter finish their coffee. They collect buckets, and call the children.

"You can't swim yet," they tell the children. "You just ate breakfast. And you have a job to do. We need to collect shellfish for tonight."

Down on the beach the tide is out. The children walk across the wet sand, and into the shallow water. They can feel the shellfish under their feet. Sometimes they can see the white and brown shells of the pipi and tuatua. They pull the shellfish out of the sand and put them in the buckets. When they are full enough, Doug and Peter carry the buckets up to the house.

They wash all the sand from the shells with clean water and fill the buckets with water from the outside tap. They leave the shellfish to soak in fresh water in the outside shower. It is cool there.

"Swim! Swim!" shout the children.

"OK. We'll come with you," say their parents. Kath and Ted go too.

The children stay in the water until lunchtime. After everyone has eaten, Kath sits in front of the house with a book. The men have gone to play golf. Marie and Joanne have taken their garden chairs down onto the sand so that they can relax, and watch the children at the same time.

Later, there will be food to prepare for the Christmas Eve BBQ, and for tomorrow, but for now Kath has nothing to do.

She watches her grandchildren. She likes doing this.

Eleven-year-old Stephanie and ten-year-old Tim are throwing a Frisbee. Wills and Jamie are only seven, and are more interested in getting dirty. They are digging a channel down the beach, and are covered in sand from head to foot.

They will need another swim and a shower before we can let them in the house, Kath smiles to herself.

Amy and Beth have built a sand castle. Beth is collecting shells and delivering them to Amy, who is using them to decorate the castle.

Kath stares. There is another child with them. A little boy is also collecting shells. Beth is six, but this boy is younger. He picks up one shell at a time, and takes it to Amy.

He can't be more than three or four years old, thinks Kath. *Where are his parents?*

Marie comes up from the beach.

"It is so hot. I need a cold drink," says Marie. "And I need more sunscreen for the kids."

"Who is that little boy?" asks Kath.

"I don't know. He says his name is David. Joanne and I looked up and down the beach. We can't see anyone else. He doesn't have a sunhat either. I'll take one down for him."

"Someone must be looking for him." Kath is worried.

"I know. But if they look on the beach, they will see him. We're watching him. He is quite safe with us."

Later, when the sun is not so strong, the children go swimming again. The little boy, David, doesn't go in the water. He sits next to

Joanne's chair and plays with the sand.

Kath takes drinks and snacks down to the beach for the children. They are hungry and thirsty. The little boy eats a lot. Kath thinks he is about three years old.

"Where do you live?" she asks him.

David waves his hand towards the north end of the beach.

"Who is at your house?"

"Nana," says the little boy.

Kath remembers there is a small holiday cottage about 200m along the beach. It is on another road. Kath doesn't know who owns it, but she guesses that David must be staying there.

"It's time to go home," she says to David. "Your Nana will be looking for you."

She calls to Stephanie and Tim. "Take David home, will you? He's staying at that cottage along the beach."

"OK," says Stephanie. "I wonder why no-one has been looking for him."

"I don't know. But please make sure it is the right house, and make sure he gets into the house safely."

Stephanie holds David's hand, and they walk away down the beach with Tim. The little boy is tired. Tim stops. He kneels down and talks to David. Then he lifts David onto Stephanie's back. Kath watches until the children turn away from the sea and walk up into the sand dunes.

Kath goes back to the beach house. When Stephanie and Tim come back, she asks them "Was everything OK?"

"I think so," answers Stephanie.

"Did you go into the cottage? Did you see anyone?"

"No. When we got there, David wanted to climb down from my back."

"He said 'Nana wakes up now. Tea. Toilet'. Then he ran into the house. He seemed very happy."

"The door was open. We could hear music. It was a TV or a radio. There was a table on the deck in front of the house with drinks and things on it," says Tim.

Kath thanks the children for taking David home, but she is still worried. *Something is strange,* she thinks. *Who would leave such a small child alone? One of us adults should have gone with him.*

When Ted gets back from golf, she talks to him about it.

"Stop worrying so much," says Ted. "You can see the beach from that house. Maybe someone was watching him playing with the children the whole time. Don't you have some food to get ready for tonight? I'm really hungry."

Sunday Night
They have a wonderful Christmas Eve BBQ.

First they cook the shellfish on a big sheet of iron. As the shells open, they throw them into a bowl with a little butter, lemon juice, and herbs. Then Peter and Doug take the iron plate off the BBQ and put the grill on. They cook lamb chops for everyone. Marie, Joanne and Kath have baked potatoes, and they have made four different salads. For dessert, Kath serves strawberries and ice cream.

It's too far to go to church, but Peter brings out his guitar. They sing Christmas carols together.

By 10:00pm, all the children are in bed. The adults are pleased. They still have a lot to do. They never have a Christmas tree at the beach house. In front of the house there is an old pohutakawa tree. It's covered in red flowers. Every year, very early in the morning, they put the children's' presents under the tree. Marie and Joanne will hang bright red cloth bags filled with small presents, on the branches. There will be one bag for each child. The younger children believe that these are from Santa. The older children know that they are from their parents. But they say they believe in Santa because they love to get Santa sacks.

Marie and Joanne are sitting at the table inside the house. They are filling the Santa sacks with fruit, candy, and small games. The girls will also get hair ribbons and bracelets, and the boys will get crazy sunglasses and water pistols. Each child will also get a book.

Suddenly, the door opens, and Beth comes in.

"Beth!" says Marie. "What are you doing up?"

"Toilet," says Beth. She disappears down the hallway towards the bathroom.

When she comes back, she asks for a drink.

Marie gives Beth a glass of milk. She sits on the sofa and has her drink.

She sees the bags on the table. "What are you doing with the Santa sacks? Where is Santa?"

"Uh, Santa came early. He has a lot to do tonight. He is so busy, he asked us to hang them on the tree for you," says Doug.

"Oh, OK." Beth is half asleep. Then she looks at the table again. She counts on her fingers. "Santa will have to come back."

"Why?" asks her mother.

"There are only six. Where's David's Santa sack?" Beth is worried.

"Santa will take David's sack to his house," says Kath.

"No. David is here. He's staying with us."

"No, Beth. He's at his house with his Nana."

"He's here. I talked to him. He has his bag and everything."

"She's been dreaming," says Marie.

Kath is not so sure.

"What did he say, dear?" Kath asks Beth.

"He doesn't talk much. He said 'Nana still sleeping. David sleeps here'."

"Then where is he? We didn't see him."

"I took him to the boys' tent. Then I came in here to go to the toilet."

Kath takes a torch from a shelf near the door. She runs outside with Marie and Joanne. They open the tent and look inside. Tim, Wills and Jamie are all asleep, and so is David. He is lying between the twins. He is wearing the same clothes he was wearing on the beach. His legs are scratched and dirty. His face is dirty too. He has been crying. There is a very small backpack lying on the floor of the tent.

Marie picks it up and opens it. Kath shines the torch inside. David has packed a sun hat, a packet of biscuits, and two small toy cars.

"Oh, no!" whispers Kath. "Something's not right! I knew it!"

They run back inside to talk to the others. The adults move quickly.

Peter, Doug and Joanne take torches and hurry along the beach to the cottage. They are sure something is very wrong. They don't know what they will find at the cottage, but Joanne is a nurse. She will know what to do.

Marie and Kath stay at the house. Beth has fallen asleep on the sofa. Marie carries her back to the caravan. They decide that they will let David sleep. They think he will be very upset if they wake him up. Marie creeps into the tent. She washes David's face very gently and covers him with a blanket.

"Poor little boy," she says to Kath.

The Cottage

The door of the cottage is open. They hurry up the steps, and into the house. There are no lights on. A radio is playing. Doug finds the light switches. He turns on the lights. There is no one in the living room. Presents are piled up under a Christmas tree. Someone was reading a magazine. Everything looks normal. Joanne goes to the kitchen. The refrigerator door is open. There is milk on the floor, and half-eaten cake on the table. *David,* she thinks. *He must have tried to get something to eat.*

"Joanne! Here!" shouts Doug. "The bedroom!"

Doug and Peter have found David's grandmother. She is lying on a bed. Her face is very white, and still. Her hair is covered in blood.

Joanne hurries to the bed. She leans over and gently examines her.

"Is she dead?" asks Peter.

"No," answers Joanne. "But she is very bad. We need help. And we need it very quickly. Doug, call an ambulance. Call the police too. I'm sure this is an accident, but we might need the police to help. Peter, they will want some information. Can you find out who she is? They will want to contact relatives."

Doug takes out his mobile phone. He talks to the emergency services. He explains what they have found.

"They want to talk to you," he says to Joanne. He gives her the phone.

Joanne tells the emergency services as much as she can. "I think the head wound is the only injury. But it is very bad. We think she has been unconscious for at least nine hours."

Peter has searched the house. He comes back into the bedroom. "I found her driver's license. Her name is Adeline Foster. She's sixty-three years old. She lives in Auckland."

Peter takes the phone. He gives the emergency services people the information.

When the call is ended, he tells Doug and Joanne. "They'll call us back when they've decided what to do. The nearest hospital is fifty kilometres away, and it's only a country hospital. They think they should take Mrs Foster to Auckland, so they will send a helicopter. They'll call back to tell us what to do."

"I hope they hurry," says Joanne. "I can't do anything to help her."

They stand and look down at the woman on the bed. She looks very ill.

"What happened?" asks Peter.

Doug points to the ceiling of the room. Peter can see a string of gold stars. The string is taped to the ceiling at one end, but the other end is hanging down.

"She climbed up to hang Christmas decorations on the ceiling. I think she fell. When she fell, she must have hit her head on the edge of the bed."

Doug's phone rings.

He answers it. "Yes?" he says. Someone speaks for a long time. Doug listens and nods. "OK. Yes we can do that."

"The police are coming now. They are bringing a doctor with them. They will arrive in about thirty minutes. A rescue helicopter is flying from Auckland. It can't land on the road because of the trees and the power lines. They will land on the beach. They have asked us to put some lights out there. They might need some help to carry Mrs Foster across the dunes and down to the beach."

Doug calls Marie and tells her everything.

Marie and Ted leave the beach house. They go to the cottage to help.

Kath stays alone with the children. She feels restless inside the house. She gets a jacket and a garden chair. She takes her telephone. She sits outside between the caravan and the tent. She watches the beach. Soon she sees lights. People are moving around. They are putting markers and lights on the hard sand near the water. An hour later the helicopter arrives. It makes a lot of noise. Kath is amazed that the children don't wake up.

She can see people climb out of the helicopter. They run up the beach carrying a stretcher. She sees them come back. She sees Joanne walking next to the stretcher. The stretcher is loaded onto the helicopter. The emergency staff climbs on too. Everyone else moves back. The helicopter rises in the air and is gone. It was on the ground for only 15 minutes.

It is almost 1:00am when everyone returns. Peter is carrying a big box wrapped in Christmas paper. Two policemen and the local doctor come too.

"We need to check on the little boy," they say.

Kath opens the tent. "He is very young," says one of the

policemen. "It's a pity, but we'll have to wake him up and take him with us."

"No," says Kath. "Leave him here. We'll look after him until his family can come."

"We can't do that," says the other policeman. "There are rules. We'll take him to a children's home. We're looking for his parents. When we find them, they will come to the children's home to get him."

"No," says Ted. "I agree with my wife. "It's better if he stays with us."

The doctor says, "David seems to be fine. Why not leave him with these people?"

Just then, one of the policemen gets a call. He walks away from the tent and talks for a few minutes. He comes back. We have found the parents. David's father is on the phone now. He says we should take David away."

"Can I talk to David's father please?" asks Kath.

The policeman hands her the phone.

Kath talks to David's father. Then she gives the phone back. "David's parents planned to drive to the beach on Christmas morning. Now they are going to the hospital in Auckland. They want to know about Mrs Foster's condition. David's father will drive here tomorrow, as soon as he can. He says it's OK. David can stay here."

The policemen check with David's father. Then they walk back to the cottage with the doctor to collect their car.

Kath has made coffee. Everyone sits down. "What did the doctor say?" she asks Joanne.

"He thinks Mrs Foster will be OK. But he said she was very lucky. If we hadn't found her she would have died before morning. She will have an emergency operation in Auckland as soon as she arrives at the hospital. "

"Peter? What is that present you are carrying?" asks Marie.

"Look," answers Peter. He shows everyone, the box. The label says, 'To David, Love Nana'."

Peter puts it on the table with the other presents. Joanne and Marie quickly take some small things from each child's Santa sack. They make a Santa sack for David. Then they go to bed.

Christmas Day

Kath goes to bed very late, but she sets the alarm and gets up at 4:00am. She takes all the presents outside and puts them under the pohutakawa tree. She hangs the Santa sacks on the branches and goes back to bed.

Of course, the children wake up when the sun rises. They run to the tree and take the Santa sacks. They know they can't touch the big presents under the tree until their parents are awake.

When Kath and Marie get up at 7:00am, the children are sitting in the living room playing their new games or reading the books from Santa. Wills and Jamie have been eating chocolate.

"Where is David?" asks Kath.

"He's still asleep," says Wills. "I didn't know he was staying here."

"No," answers Kath. "Neither did we. But it's OK. His grandmother had an accident. She's in hospital, so David will stay with us until his father can come."

She tells the children about the policemen and the doctor and the helicopter. They are all very angry with her.

"There was a helicopter on the beach?"

"And you didn't wake us up!"

"Stop thinking about the helicopter. Start thinking about little David and his poor grandmother!" she says to them.

"Sorry, Gran," says Tim. "Shall I go and see if David's awake?"

"I'll come with you," says Kath.

They go outside. David's awake. He's still in the tent. He's crying. "Nana. Where's Nana?"

"Come on love," says Kath. "You'll see Nana soon. Come out and see what Santa brought you."

Tim crawls into the tent and brings David out. He holds David's hand and takes him over to the pohutakawa tree. He helps David pull the Santa sack off the tree.

David stops crying. He holds the bag tightly.

I'll have to clean him up before his father sees him, thinks Kath. *I wonder if I can get into the cottage and find him some clean clothes?*

Back in the house, Marie takes croissants from the freezer and starts making coffee.

By the time everyone is out of bed, showered and dressed, the tables are up outside the house, loaded with Christmas breakfast.

When everyone is sitting and eating, Beth starts picking up the presents from under the tree. She gives them to everyone. She can't read very well, so Amy has to help her.

Amy helps David unwrap the present from his grandmother. It is a big truck. David is delighted.

Doug gets a phone call from David's father. His mother-in-law, Mrs Foster, is out of danger. His wife will stay with her, but he is leaving Auckland to drive down and collect David.

It's another beautiful day. For lunch they eat some of the big Christmas ham, with green peas and tiny boiled potatoes. They are playing cricket on the beach when David's father arrives. He runs along the beach from the cottage. At first, he can't see his son. Will and Jamie are teaching David how to hold a cricket bat.

"David!" shouts his father. "David!" He runs and picks up his son. "Thank God, you're all right!"

He turns to the family. "I can't thank you enough."

"Oh, don't worry about that. Come up to the house and have something to eat and drink," says Ted.

Kath makes sandwiches and coffee. David's father eats and drinks. He is very tired. He sits on the sofa, and falls asleep with David in his arms.

It is late in the afternoon when he leaves. He straps David into his car seat. This is difficult, because David does not want to let go of his truck.

He stands at the door of his car. "You did so much for us. Without you, my mother-in-law might have died. And you looked after David like your own child."

"We didn't do anything special. We are so sorry we didn't see that there was a problem earlier. We hope that your mother-in-law will soon be well. Please give our best wishes to Mrs Foster, and to your wife. We hope we see David here at the beach again. He's a lovely little boy, and he is very brave," says Ted.

The family stands out on the road and waves until the car is out of sight.

The others go back down to the beach to swim, but Kath stays in the house. She looks at the kitchen. There are mountains of dishes waiting to be washed.

Do I really love Christmas? she wonders. *After another hour or two, everyone will be hungry again. Oh well. It's family. That's what Christmas is about.*

She hears someone coming into the house. It's Ted. "Why don't you sit down and relax? Pete, Doug and I will wash the dishes."

THANK YOU

Thank you for reading Stories for Christmas. (Word count: 10,088)
We hope you enjoyed it.

If you would like to read more graded readers, please visit our
website http://www.italkyoutalk.com

Other Level 3 graded readers include
A Dangerous Weekend
A Holiday to Remember
Akiko and Amy Part 1
Akiko and Amy Part 2
Akiko and Amy Part 3
Be My Valentine
Different Seas
Enjoy Your Business Trip
Enjoy Your Homestay
I Need a Friend
Old Jack's Ghost Stories from England (1)
Old Jack's Ghost Stories from England (2)
Old Jack's Ghost Stories from Ireland
Old Jack's Ghost Stories from Japan
Old Jack's Ghost Stories from Scotland
Old Jack's Ghost Stories from Wales
Party Time!
The Curse

Together Again
Who is Holly?

ABOUT THE AUTHOR

I Talk You Talk Press is a Japan-based publisher of language textbooks, graded readers and language learning/teaching resources.

Our team is made up of highly experienced language teachers and translators, who have all studied at least one additional language to an advanced level.

This experience enables us to design our materials from the perspective of both the teacher and the learner. We consult with both teachers and language learners when designing our textbooks and graded readers, and test our materials extensively in the classroom before publication.

We are a fast-growing press, and currently publish graded readers for learners of English. We publish new graded readers monthly.

www.ingramcontent.com/pod-product-compliance
Lightning Source LLC
Chambersburg PA
CBHW022348040426
42449CB00006B/783